Space

A Journey to Whole Being

Space

A Journey To Whole Being

Marguerite A. Jenkin

CONTENTS

Introduction: The Space Mission

M y hope is that this simple book will help you fully enjoy your space on earth, and bring you a sense of finally coming home to yourself. Perhaps you feel a little uncomfortable or insecure in your own skin? Or maybe you have lost, or never really found, a sense of meaning and purpose to life? Perhaps you're not sure if you deserve to be happy or successful, and wonder from time to time why you seem unable to fully connect with the love and joy life has to offer? Maybe you feel frustrated and disappointed in yourself, your relationships, your whole life even?

Or maybe you're holding on so tight you've forgotten who you really are. You're not alone. We all get to feel this sometimes, to greater or lesser degrees, it just seems to be part of our human nature and our human journey. But it doesn't always have to be this way.

In fact we don't have to travel far to travel a very long way on our life's journey. Yes we can and do make life tiresome and a burden by carrying a lot of unnecessary baggage, just in case. Or maybe others gave us some of their bags to carry for a while, without really asking or meaning to. Perhaps we get a bit lost sometimes and go the long way round, or we don't even know where the destination is anyhow. It doesn't matter. Starting now, starting anywhere, we can begin to choose for ourselves a lighter more spacious existence. Honestly.

It's all about allowing yourself a feeling of space inside and out, and with that simple process comes awareness, acceptance, an aliveness, a freedom, a sense of joy, connection, completeness, and other nice things like that, though not necessarily in that order, or maybe all at once. Becoming more physically sensitive to your own spaciousness, and focussing your attention and imagination on your inner and outer experience of being in the world, brings a welcome sense of wholeness. It can change the quality of your life and relationships for the better.

And it's actually easy, though that in itself presents a challenge to our preconceptions of how things should be. You don't have to make a long and arduous pilgrimage to get to the destination of self-knowledge and self-acceptance, unless it gives you a greater sense of achievement. You just have to be here and on the journey.

Don't worry about how far you've come and how far there is to go, it would be pointless and constricting. It's often much easier to walk around the mountain of self-judgement or the huge crater of regret, or anything else we might like to put in our own way. They're often a lot smaller than you think. In any case, I'm not sure any of us ever finally arrive anywhere, we just continue to explore the way with a greater sense of our own potential and life's exciting possibilities, which has to be more fun. So let's both forget the journey thing for now. I'm sorry I mentioned it. This book is about being simply and fully present in space, but with both feet on the ground.

I truly hope you find something in this book that speaks to you, but trust what feels right and then feel free to throw away the rest. As you'll see, I have suggested some techniques to increase awareness of our sense of inner and outer space, but just reading about and focussing attention on the concept of the space in and around you can somehow bring a sense of expansion to your being, which can help to make you feel more whole. This book is a reminder of what you probably already know. It's not rocket science and it's not weird. It's about remembering that your space to be you is your birthright and yours for the taking right now. Yes you.

The Rocket Launch

Part I: INNER SPACE

1. The Spacesuit: Cells that Breathe

Our human bodies are made up of a countless number of cells which are the building blocks of all living organisms, and they come in a variety of specialist types such as skin, brain, muscle, and blood. Many cells cluster together in sociable communities, making up organs and bones; whilst others such as blood or sperm cells are individual in nature, though in the case of the latter very sociable given the right circumstances.

Although they vary in shape, type and function, each cell has three main parts: a flexible outer wall, the plasma membrane; a nucleus which acts as the cell's control centre containing our DNA and managing the cellular functions; and between those two parts is the third, cytoplasm, which contains smaller molecules (including proteins, amino acids and fatty acids) which perform the cellular functions that support life.

Cells are basically made up of water (about three quarters) and energy (stored nutrients and the machinery to metabolise those nutrients so the cells can carry out their roles). There is fluid in the space within the cells and in the spaces between the cells. The cells themselves breathe, taking in oxygen and nutrients and expelling wastes through the porous breathable membrane. Simply put, to allow healthy development and functioning, our cells are energised and nourished by the air that we breathe, the water that we drink, and the food that we eat. They are also very clever.

I'm only mentioning all this so you can get an idea of how all human life, from the smallest cell, to the communities of cells which make up our organs, tissues and bones, right up to the level of our whole being, needs the space to breathe, the space to expand and contract. These cells are the building blocks that make up our physical bodies and form the wonderful space suit that we wear in this world. Cells contain space, and are themselves contained by and move within a wider space. In the same way, we as individuals are made up of space and are moving within space. To be healthy we need to allow ourselves an unrestricted and expansive freedom to breathe.

Here is a lovely illustration of human cells, but being of

Human Cells

rather simple mind and inclination, I prefer to imagine our human cells as a bunch of brightly coloured balloons, lightly held together but with tiny spaces between them. They each contain space and energy (hot air), and although their outer skin is flexible they take their rightful space in balloon form (they are not squashed and constricted), and move gently in the space around them. The strings and bow are optional. These are your cells and they are dancing within you. Become aware of them and they breathe more deeply.

Human Cells (in balloon form)

2. The Starfish: Love and Acceptance

Enough talk for now. Find a quiet room, clear a large comfortable space on the floor, and lie down on your back in a starfish shape – arms out at your sides at shoulder height, palms up; and legs in a wide v-shape, feet falling out, eyes closed. Make sure you are warm, so cover yourself with a blanket if you need to. If your neck is uncomfortable then place a small cushion or book underneath your head. Remember this is your space and you deserve every inch of it.

Become aware of your back and pelvis on the floor and move a little against the floor, like a dog rolling on its back in the grass in the sunshine. Come to stillness and let the slight curve in your lower back sink towards the ground. Become aware of your hands and wiggle your fingers. Become aware of the backs of your hands resting on the floor, your fingers lightly curved upwards. Become aware of the whole length between the fingertips of your left and right hands, and feel the space widen across your back. Your shoulders are falling into the ground.

Become aware of your feet and wiggle your toes, letting your legs, knees and feet fall out to the side. Your legs feel long and loose. Feel your pelvis resting on the floor, rock it slightly from top to bottom and then side to side, enjoying the contact with the ground. Come again to stillness and be aware of the space within your pelvis, sensing how this space connects your legs in a u-shape from left foot to right foot, and right foot to left.

If your lower back feels uncomfortable in this position then plant both feet flat on the floor, about hip-width apart, and about a thigh's length away from your buttocks, with your knees pointing upwards. You can either continue your exploration in this way or move from one position to the other from time to time, depending on what is comfortable for you and how your body feels most at ease.

Imagine your head as the fifth point of the Starfish and become aware of the spaciousness of your neck. Gently roll your head slightly left to right, keeping contact with the ground all the while. Imagine the back of your neck lengthening, feeling free and loose. An inner movement may follow this thought, but don't consciously force your body into a new position or into being right or wrong, just give it space. Let the back of your head and the back of your lovely long neck melt into the floor.

Now become aware of the space connecting the different points of your Starfish – left foot to right hand, left hand to right foot, head to right foot, head to left hand, right hand to left hand, left foot to left hand, and so on and so on, whatever combinations you like. Move your awareness slowly from one to the other, giving each of the connections length and space and time. Bask in this sense of spaciousness and freedom.

Become quietly still but feel your whole body alive. This is your space. Imagine every part of you that is touching the floor enjoying the floor, being supported by the floor, flowing freely into the floor – the backs of your hands, the backs of your arms, your wide shoulders and long spine, the back of your head, your buttocks, your pelvis, the coccyx at the base of your spine, the outer sides of your feet, and the length of your legs. The ground is holding you, welcoming you, supporting you.

The Starfish

When you feel ready, turn your attention inwards. Ask yourself, where am I holding any tension? My jaw? My tongue? My forehead? My neck? My shoulders? My chest? The backs of my legs? My eyes? My feet? The space between my eyebrows? My solar plexus? My pelvis? Those are some favourites but go wherever your attention takes you, wherever you feel a holding or contraction or tightness, and imagine giving that area the space to breathe. In your mind's eye see this part of you gently expanding and contracting like a breath. You may feel it melt or give a little with the attention, see if you can go with it, and allow any release or movement to happen gently.

Your breathing may deepen slightly, just notice and allow the breath to breathe in and out, nothing is forced, nothing needs to be changed. You may feel some anxiety or perhaps a rising sense of excitement, just try and lovingly stay with whatever sensations arise, for as short or long a while as is comfortable, continuing to bring a quality of soft expansion and space. Your mind will probably wander from time to time, but gently bring your attention back to the same area of holding in the body, imagining a physical feeling of spaciousness, or perhaps silently saying the word space...space...space...space...space slowly over and over in your mind. Or maybe you've fallen asleep?

Or imagine the part of you that feels tight and tense as a gloriously coloured balloon, or bunch of balloons, and see them full and free, floating lightly and gently in the breeze. Or in your mind's eye picture the human cells making up that area of your body, connected in wonderful patterns of togetherness, and bring space to those cells, within them and between them, so they become comfortably expansive and alive. Experiment and explore with whatever way seems to work best for you.

If you feel an easing of tension, or feel a sense of aliveness and energy, or even if you don't, then perhaps try allowing that same part of you even more space for a short while, or simply enjoy resting there. There are no limits, no rules, no need for judgements or worries about getting it right or getting it wrong. Just stay for however long feels right for you, or until your mind wanders again, as it surely will, then gently move your attention to another area of your body where you've discovered holding and repeat the same process. You are taking a trip around the body searching for any areas of tension or discomfort that call to you, giving them attention, bringing space and freedom, and allowing them to breathe.

If it helps you, picture your attention as an astronaut, an intrepid space explorer who is travelling from place to place, planet to planet, in a lovely silver space rocket. And, whenever you feel like it or feel drawn to something, get out and explore, have a good look around. Imagine bringing a sense of spaciousness and expansion wherever you land, take a few photographs, and then climb back into your rocket and set off again. Give yourself permission to be childlike in your curiosity and enjoy exploring. Boldly go where you haven't gone before.

If you don't find yourself particularly drawn to different parts of your body, or any areas of tightness, then why not just travel gently from your head, to your neck, to your shoulders, to your arms, your hands, to your chest, to your back, your solar plexus, your pelvis, your legs, to your feet. Resting freely in each and bringing the quality of space until you feel ready to move on. You may well be saying to yourself that you can't feel anything, but your sensitivity will build with practice so

The Lovely Silver Space Rocket & the Astronaut

keep gently trying, bringing the qualities of spaciousness and ease, of freedom and fullness, wherever you are focussing your attention. If this sounds a little repetitive that's because it is, but it can also be endlessly fascinating. That's because you are in fact endlessly fascinating, and there is so much to learn about you, but with no judgement, just openness, curiosity and space.

If you become irritable or bored or tired, or just plain fidgety, then bring your curiosity and awareness to that feeling. Ask yourself where the irritation or boredom is being physically felt in your body and move your attention to that place. Or perhaps ask your astronaut to go and have a little look around. Imagine bringing a sense of spaciousness there, allowing that part of you to be free and to simply breathe. Let it be. See if you can let yourself fully feel and experience what is going on, if only for a moment.

Perhaps this feeling needs to be expressed somehow, maybe you feel like roaring with rage or frustration, then see if you can allow yourself to do just that, a good bellow might help. No need to ask yourself why, no need to get caught up in thinking, analysis or judgement. No need to try and get it right (whatever that is), simply see if you can stay with the physical sensations for a moment. Then return to your exploration, turning your attention inwards once more and asking yourself, where is the holding in my body now?

If you are criticising yourself for not doing it right, then take your attention to your head and imagine bringing lightness and space to the cells in your busy brain. There is no right and wrong here, there's just attention and space. No need to change anything, or force your brain to relax or to be something it's not. Just give your brain cells the space to breathe. You can even sigh if it helps – aaaaaaaaaaaaahhhhhhh – as long as you like, quietly or loudly, musically or in a tuneless monotone, whatever takes your fancy, it feels pretty good.

Continue to explore your body for as long as feels comfortable for you, sometimes bringing the sense of spaciousness to specific areas of holding, sometimes bringing the sense of spaciousness to your body as a whole, and all the while allowing this space, your space, to feel alive, expansive and free. As you become aware of the spaciousness within, there will often follow an expansion and deepening of the breath, perhaps only momentarily, but just observe, no need to change anything, or to force yourself to keep breathing deeply.

Remember that the quality of this sense of space you are bringing is love, a loving acceptance of your experience of yourself rather than a rejection of how things are for you. You are not denying or constricting or changing your experience, but observing what you find and giving it space, space, and more space, without judgement, without striving for it to be anything other than how it is for you right now. Try saying to yourself as you lie in this Starfish position the simple words 'I AM HERE', letting your whole body absorb the words, sense the power of the words, and repeat the phrase a few times, silently or out loud, just noticing how you feel.

To bring this journey into space to a close, move your legs closer together, slightly less than hip-width apart, feet falling out, and your arms down by your sides palms up. Just listen to your breath, no need for forced deepening, simply listen to it, feel the expansion and contraction of your belly, like the movement of waves on a shore. Be aware of your body as a whole being, enjoy the aliveness within, and then gently take your attention

The Corpse Posture

to feel the air on your skin, your back on the floor. Listen to the sounds around you, become aware of the light in the room, and finally open your eyes. In yoga, this is cheerfully called the 'Corpse Posture', but you should feel very alive. It is a little more contained than the Starfish, and staying with this for a couple of minutes after your space trip should help ground you as you gradually come back to Earth.

You don't really need to read the rest of this book. Just giving yourself the opportunity to do the Starfish once or twice a day will allow you to develop a sense of your inner space, the space that is rightfully yours. It is from this place that a greater sense of aliveness and comfortableness in being manifests itself. Don't worry if you fall asleep, that's fine, the body probably needed rest, but practising focussing your attention on areas of tension, on your inner experience, will build your ability to stay awake. Enjoy it. You deserve the time to revel in your own space. There is so much to explore. You can do this for as long or short a time as you like, but if you choose to spend ten minutes on it each day that really is a great start.

3. Space Exploration: Body, Mind, Emotions

You might be wondering what this is all about. How on earth is doing the Starfish space trip everyday going to make you happy and more comfortable in your own skin? A good question. Well, it's really a very simple but effective way to start to become more fully aware of how we actually feel inside, and to give ourselves permission to be still, to listen to and fully inhabit our body using our physical senses and imagination.

To find out who we are we have to listen to ourselves, to get to know ourselves, to give ourselves time and attention. In fact, many of us will have spent years running away from ourselves, keeping relentlessly busy, or just switching off, all to avoid thinking about what we truly want, or to avoid being who we truly are. Listening to our body, giving it our undivided attention and bringing a sense of spaciousness, curiosity and acceptance, can reveal how we really think and feel. Listening to our body can reveal our hopes and fears, our joys and sadness. Our body is really very clever, and it deserves to be given the space to speak and to be heard. You are worth getting to know. It's not selfish to be interested in what you have to say, it is natural and healthy. Remember that you are worth exploring.

As you start to experiment with the Starfish and give yourself time to travel around your body bringing attention and space, you may notice that what starts as a physical experience often gives rise to wandering thoughts or a variety of feelings. Sometimes you will get completely distracted, caught up in your mind, absorbed in your thinking. Perhaps you are criticising how you are doing the exercise, or worrying about the day ahead, thinking about what you want for dinner, or just daydreaming. Simply notice these thoughts, observe them, and ask yourself, what effect are these thoughts having on my body?

Maybe self-critical thoughts are bringing a sense of tension to your solar plexus; maybe thoughts of all the work you need to do today causes your brow to furrow and your forehead and shoulders to tense; maybe you're getting confused and your head's beginning to ache. Just notice, and gently bring your attention to this bodily sensation and give it space, imagining the cells in that part of you breathing freely and fully. No need for judgement. Once you've noticed the thoughts, there's no need to get caught in them and let them spin around and around. Just keep bringing your attention and a physical feeling of spaciousness back to the part of your body that speaks to you. There is no right or wrong. Just notice.

Sometimes you will become aware of how you are feeling as you lie in the Starfish, in an emotional rather than a physical sense. It may be a feeling directly related to the thoughts going through your head. Or it could be a feeling that seems to be there for no immediately obvious reason, a wave of emotion that just seems to come over you for a moment. Perhaps you're experiencing a general sense of anxiety or sadness, or perhaps a sudden flush of anger or frustration. As before, whatever is there for you, whatever you become aware of, just notice. No need for judgement. No need to try and change anything.

Ask yourself, what is the bodily sensation associated with this? Where am I experiencing this emotional feeling in my body? Perhaps your feeling of sadness is related to a tightness in your chest, or maybe you are feeling nervous and excited, with a buzzing sensation in your solar plexus or pelvis? Go to that part of your body in your mind's eye, bringing a sense of space, imagining the cells breathing fully and freely, whilst also allowing yourself to release and give space to any emotions that are passing through.

Of course it can take courage and determination to continue to give the physical expression of those feelings space. But you have that strength within you and so, if only for a moment, allow your feelings to be fully present in the body. There's no need to get caught up in the feelings themselves and let them overwhelm you, no need to get caught up in analysing the story behind the feelings, just notice what is happening. As you bring spaciousness to the part of the body that speaks to you, there may be a physical release of emotions, see if you can just let them be free and flow through. Give yourself permission, give yourself the space.

Maybe you feel like crying, so you let yourself cry, give the crying space. Maybe you feel like roaring with anger, so you let yourself roar, give the anger space. Maybe you feel like

Space Exploration

moaning, or sighing, or laughing. Just explore. Whatever it is, it will pass and release, it's all completely normal, no rights or wrongs, no time limitations, nothing to feel ashamed of. Keep gently bringing back your attention to the physical spaciousness in your body, imagining the cells breathing gently, full and free. Or if it feels too much to stay any longer in this place, then don't, just gently allow yourself to move on.

It might cheer you up to know that it's not all doom and gloom of course, sometimes more obviously positive feelings such as joy or hope or excitement may arise, but it can also take courage to continue to give those feelings space. You deserve to feel loving, joyous, hopeful, calm or content, whatever it might be, but perhaps this challenges your own preconceptions about your own worth. As before, locate this feeling in the body, then go there in your mind's eye, exploring the physical sensations and bringing a sense of space, imagining the cells breathing fully and freely, whilst also allowing yourself to be present to, and give space to, any emotions that are simply passing through.

So as you continue to practise the Starfish, exploring areas of holding and tension in the body may reveal hidden thoughts and emotions which call for your attention; and vice versa, perhaps thoughts and emotions may arise of themselves and reveal areas of deep holding and tension in the body. You can choose which direction to take, you can choose which areas to explore, and for how long. Whatever feels right for you. And wherever you go, you take with you the qualities of spaciousness, openness, curiosity and acceptance.

As you build your sensitivity and awareness, you may experience a wide variety of physical sensations, perhaps tension, or stiffness, or aching, or hardness, or softness, or heat, or cold, perhaps a tingling or a buzzing energy. The sensation may be a little uncomfortable or it may be a little pleasurable. There shouldn't however be any physically painful sensations, so take care of yourself and trust yourself to know when you ought to stop or move on. As you explore, you might feel these physical sensations in your throat, your chest, your solar plexus, your pelvis, your sexual organs, your legs, or maybe on the top of your head. You might feel something over a broad area or as a more precise pin prick of discomfort in your finger tip. However these physical sensations manifest for you, just notice and give the sensation space, imagining the cells in that part of your body spacious and free. There is no right or wrong here, it's all an exploration, and as a unique individual, you have a whole universe of your own to explore.

Sometimes, when you bring attention and space to a part of your body which reveals or reflects a particular feeling or thought, you may notice a shift in that thought or feeling, just as you may notice a shift in the physical sensation from tension to ease. Feelings of sadness may transform to calm, feelings of anger may transform to sadness, feelings of joy may transform to melancholy, self-critical thoughts may transform to thoughts of self-acceptance, busy thoughts may transform to a mind empty of thoughts. Interesting isn't it? Always changing.

And then again sometimes there is no transformation. So, we have to determinedly keep bringing our attention back to the same physical sensation and feel the same sadness or whatever is there, and give it as much space as we can muster on that day and then move on. Some days you will feel deeply and other days you may feel nothing. Remember though that sometimes great things can come from nothing and the day when you think 'Why am I bothering to do this?' may be the day when something changes and the practice deepens. Or it may not. Just enjoy exploring.

4. Space Exploration: A History of the Universe

Your body is your universe. Whatever your physical appearance, your physical health, or your spiritual belief or non-belief, there is no arguing with the fact that your body contains a wealth of information to explore. It is the living and breathing expression of our personal journey in this world and of where we are on that journey here and now.

The body remembers our experiences in a way the mind sometimes forgets. That's why a certain smell, like newly cut grass, or a particular perfume, or the scent of a bonfire on an autumn night, can transport you back in time in an instant. Or why imagining the feel of sand between your toes, or holding a loved one's hand, or hearing a certain piece of music, can shift your mood in a moment. It's also why you can logically argue something in your mind while at the same time your body is feeling the absolute opposite. You may feel anxious in certain social situations and you don't really know the reason, but perhaps your body is remembering a particular event in your past where you felt embarrassed or shamed or unsafe in some way. You can't get rid of body memories even if they are unconscious, even if you try to push them away or ignore them, but you can give them space to breathe so your life force can flow freely in the here and now.

Our thoughts and feelings manifest themselves physically in some form big or small throughout our daily lives. Many of your thoughts have a physical beginning, basic ones such as I must have a drink of water or I must go to the toilet right away; or more complex ones such as the desire to creatively express yourself or perhaps to have children. Many of your feelings have a physical beginning and are often hormonal or chemical in origin, such as pre-menstrual tension or some forms of depression. Many of your thoughts have a corresponding physical manifestation, a frown on your face, a sudden pang of anxiety, a snort of laughter when you read a funny book or remember something your friend said last night. And many of your feelings have a physical manifestation, a stooping posture when we feel a lack of confidence or happiness, a sinking sensation in our heart when someone rejects us, a soaring sensation in our heart when we feel compassion or love for someone, or a tight feeling in our solar plexus when we feel anxious.

There are countless examples of how our thoughts and feelings are physically expressed, from basic needs and responses to more complicated scenarios, in both positive and negative manifestations, which can reveal so much about ourselves. This relationship between thinking, feeling and physicality is often reflected in the colour of our language. So we feel heartbroken, or a stab of jealousy, or describe events as stomach churning or gut wrenching, whilst the word courage translates from its French origins as angry heart, and so on.

A healthy body is one that allows the physical sensations arising from thoughts or feelings to flow through. This is what animals do. It's what enables them to live in the moment. In the natural world there is a natural flow and it is non-judgemental and sometimes brutal in the bid for survival. As human beings we are wonderfully free to make intelligent, compassionate and moral choices about our actions in the world. But to do this in a

The Universal Flow

healthy, conscious way, we need to allow ourselves to bring our awareness to what is happening within us, to give space to our experience, even if we choose not to act on it. In so doing we release the natural energetic flow within our bodies.

This energetic flow allows us to move freely, to breathe fully, and to be in touch with the universal flow of life that is constantly changing from moment to moment, like the fresh running water of a mountain stream. No moment is ever the same, as the water flows over and around hard rocks or between soft green reeds, as it dances with the rain or glistens in the sun. When we try to resist our experiences, good or bad, perhaps by shutting down emotionally or holding tension in our bodies, we are trying to narrow or stem this flow of life, which causes more tension and a sense of disconnection from ourselves and from the world.

Perhaps there are parts of us that have been denied the space to talk in the past, maybe at first by others in our personal history, but now by our own selves. Maybe there are parts of us or our experience about which we feel shame, self-judgement, anxiety, rage, overwhelm, or fearfulness, and so we push them away. We have all had bad experiences in life, and we all feel these emotions from time to time, plus other juicy ones like jealousy and grief. They are part of our human nature. But if we push them away and deny them space, we actually give them more power over us, and we can continue to carry these unacknowledged or unexpressed emotions, holding their heavy weight as tension in our bodies. And somehow or other, by denying what we perceive as negative, we also desensitise ourselves to the more obviously cuddly emotions such as joy, love and self-acceptance. Which really doesn't seem fair, does it?

When we decide to give ourselves the time and space to be still and to listen without judgement to what's there, we start to bring ourselves love and compassion maybe for the first time. We begin to free and heal ourselves. It is truly important in this process of healing to feel comfortable in our own bodies, whatever emotions are felt there, and whatever shape or size we are. When you are deeply connecting with your inner spaciousness, any concerns you may have about your external image and appearance will start to fall away and become meaningless. Developing a supportive relationship with our own self is what enables us to form good relationships with other people, and what allows us to truly release our own potential as a human being.

Children are naturally open and sensitive to their surroundings, more connected to their own experiences and emotions, and open to the emotions and behaviours of their families from whom they learn. It is part of a healthy development to adulthood to learn about oneself and the world in a safe and loving environment, and in relationship with supportive parental figures. The child begins to explore the world around him or her, and in the simplest terms to explore what feels good and what feels bad, physically and emotionally; learning appropriate responses to situations by looking to his or her parents for affirmation and encouragement, and by absorbing both their verbal and non-verbal responses. The child then gradually develops a sense of its own identity or 'self', able to safely experience itself as a being separate from mother or father. Developing a strong sense of self is an essential part of developing our full potential in life.

In reality though, we have all to a greater or lesser extent had difficult and damaging experiences in our personal history and the emotions arising from these events can be overwhelming. In developmental terms, children who experience direct or indirect abuse, who do not receive appropriate love, support and care, or who are exposed too young to damaging adult behaviour which they cannot understand, or are perhaps shamed in some way for expressing themselves, will often internalise and suppress their natural responding emotions, such as fear, grief, anger, or rage, in order to be able to cope with the situation they are in.

In other words, if it became too painful or dangerous to let ourselves feel our emotions, then a natural sense of self-preservation kicks in and we somehow unconsciously disconnect from those painful feelings or disown that vulnerable part of ourselves. Later on in life it might feel like part of us is missing. Or we might look to others to try and make us feel more whole, perhaps hanging on to unhealthy and painful relationships, when really the answer is to explore the space within.

The Flower

Where went my sense of wonder
When looking at a flower?
The fleshy feel of snap-dragon
Could occupy an hour.

Breathe deep the sharp tomato greens,
Feel red ripe fullness fruit.
Speak quietly to youthful soul,
In earth my feet take root.

Moss between the paving stones,
Sun glints on cat fur dust.
Life flows loose and loving through,
There is no need to trust.

Beauty felt as well as seen
Through skin so sweet-pea thin.
Unready then to shield the blow
Of human pain gone in.

The suppression of emotion and experience can have long-term consequences, often resulting in feelings of shame, self-blame, low self-esteem and depression. And we hold a corresponding tension in our bodies, which can lead to a sense of unworthiness, or unwellness, or maybe even illness. Perhaps we hunch our shoulders or tighten our chest to hide feelings of fear or vulnerability. Perhaps we grit our teeth or clench our jaw to block our tears or bite down our rage. Perhaps we carry tension in our pelvic area or our intestines to block feelings of revulsion, shame and guilt in relation to our sexuality or body.

We often don't realise what we are doing, we've been doing it for so long it feels familiar to us, and we think it must just be the way things are. But our connection to our physical senses and to our sense of wholeness as a person has been fractured and diminished, our sensitivities dulled. And so we can carry negative self-beliefs and physical tensions from childhood into adulthood, or develop them further in early adulthood, layer upon layer. This can have a profound impact on our ability to take our rightful place in the world, limiting the fulfilment of our potential and our ability to have healthy, nourishing relationships with others, and with the world we find ourselves in.

In fact we can become detached from our bodies, living our lives in our heads, maybe in purely intellectual pursuits; or living our lives caught in our emotions, swinging from one drama to another without any control or connection to ourselves, but with an unspecific sense of yearning for something lost. Or perhaps we are somewhere in between. Even if we don't know it, what we're really searching for is our own solid self. The good news is that we can discover a more balanced sense of who we are simply by exploring. This journey of exploration cultivates a non-judgemental awareness and acceptance of our body sensations, thoughts and emotions, which brings with it a sense of self-acceptance and ease, and a greater sense of wholeness of being.

One way we protect ourselves from the painful nature of our experiences can be the unconscious creation of a false sense of self, a pretend version of ourselves that strives to hide our vulnerability and confusion. This false sense of self is the image that we present to the world, and often to ourselves, and can manifest in a whole variety of ways, mentally, emotionally and physically. Perhaps you look strong, capable and confident but the permanent smile and rigid posture hide a real vulnerability, loneliness and distrust of others. Perhaps you seem nervous and hold yourself smaller than you are, with a quiet hesitant voice that belies your strength and passion for fear of being shamed or rejected in some way. There are so many possibilities. We may even have a few versions of this false self to fit a range of different circumstances.

The false self is our protective shell with good intentions, a suit of armour designed against attack from the outside in. Yet, if we are not aware of its existence, it can disconnect us not only from our natural sensitivity to the world around us, but also from who we truly are. In this way it attacks us from the inside out. We may also unconsciously protect ourselves by over-identifying with a certain role in life – the good mother, father, son or daughter, the employee, best-friend, joker, lover, critic, helper, rebel, whatever it might be, and in so doing neglect other aspects of our being.

Of course these are completely natural strategies for

survival and will have served us at the time of their creation. Indeed protecting ourselves is obviously practical and healthy in certain situations in our adult world, but the point is we need to be able to consciously choose our responses. If the personality we have adopted, or the armour we are wearing, is constricting us, literally affecting the way we hold our bodies, restricting our space to move and to breath, impairing our ability to make healthy choices, and to have meaningful relationships with ourselves and others, then it no longer serves us well. If we have even forgotten that we have it on and no longer know what we look like underneath, then we have some work to do. We need to get to know ourselves as we truly are. We want a spacesuit that breathes and gives us room to move and dance, not a suit of armour that constricts us, weighs us down and hides our true self.

I realise that this may all seem a bit much after the nice trip in a space rocket earlier on. But a compassionate understanding of the history of your individual universe, and the knowledge that these are experiences we all share in one way or another, helps to begin to chip away at any self-blame or negative

The Suit of Armour & the Spacesuit

self-judgement you might be carrying. It's not just you. We're all in the same space ship really. It's part of the human experience. Difficult events in life can lead us to curl up and hide in a corner and squeeze our sense of space to avoid feeling pain. At the same time though we avoid fully inhabiting our bodies, fully enjoying our senses, fully connecting with other people and taking up our rightful space in the world. Perhaps we no longer think we know how.

So the bad news is that none of us have lived in a perfect world – not you, not your parents, and not your children, despite your best efforts. The personal stories may be different, the degree of difficulty may be different, but the themes are universal. As children we couldn't do anything other than we did when faced with challenging or painful situations or emotions. We did not have the knowledge or power either to choose our experiences, or to choose how to react to those experiences. We may not consciously remember our stories, but our bodies sometimes hold on to the memories. The good news is that as adults we can relearn a way to be open and sensitive to these experiences and to reconnect with our own sense of self, perhaps for the first time. In a sense we have to begin to learn to parent ourselves, to make healthy choices for ourselves, to start to listen more deeply to our own bodies and feelings by giving ourselves the time and a safe space to explore.

To be honest, you don't have to fully understand every aspect of your own story. But it does help you start to develop compassion for, and acceptance of, yourself if you can learn about the journey you have been on so far. You don't have to get too involved in understanding the other characters in your story either. They're on their own journey. What's important here is you. Allow yourself the time to listen to your body and hear what it has to say to you in the here and now. No need to relive your story frame by frame. Sometimes memories and emotions may surface as you begin to listen to your body and practise the Starfish, and sometimes they may not. Gently keep your focus on the holding or tension in your body that needs to be given space, listened to, and released. Try and stay with the flow – thoughts, feelings, body sensations will come and go. Just tune in regularly with an open curiosity, without judgement, with compassion, and give your body space to breathe.

5. The Standing Star: Power and Will

So let's take some time now to feel the energy and power of your own unique space. Find a quiet room, kick your shoes off and stand where you have plenty of clear space around you. Stand with your legs just a little more than hip-width apart, with your feet turned slightly out. Allow your lower back to lengthen a little and tilt your pelvis ever so slightly forward so your whole back feels straight and long. Just let your arms feel long and loose by your sides, palms facing your legs. Your eyes are open and your gaze is forward and soft.

Become aware of your feet on the floor. Explore and enjoy the solidity and texture of the floor beneath them. Feel the balls of your feet connecting with the floor, your heels connecting with the floor, the sides of your feet connecting with the floor, your toes connecting with the floor. Enjoy a comfortable stretch in your feet, aware of the space within your feet, and around your feet. Curl your toes upwards, then

The Standing Star – 1

tuck your toes under, back and forth a few times. Feel the length in your toes and then spread your toes a little, aware of the spaces between them, then just wiggle your toes. It feels good. Imagine your feet enjoying the sensation of standing in soft sand, or lush green grass, or a deep fur rug. Imagine your feet like the roots of a tree reaching into the warm dark earth while the tree stands tall and strong.

Become aware of how the weight of your whole body is supported by your feet and supported by the floor. Gently move your weight from side to side, from outside edge towards the curving instep and back to the middle, then from heel to toes and back to the middle. A few times. Whatever feels right. Maybe your heels come slightly off the floor, and then your toes, and then your heels, and then your toes. Enjoy the connection with the floor and with the earth through your feet. Begin to rock just slightly on your feet by moving your weight from left foot to right foot, to left foot to right foot, alternately bending each knee slightly so your hips wiggle a little from side to side, but still keep your attention focussed in your feet. Perhaps make a movement which is quite rapid at first and then gradually allow it to become smaller and smaller until you become still. Imagine your weight evenly spread across your feet, you're not leaning forward, you're not leaning back, you're not tilting outwards, you're not tilting inwards. Your connection with the ground is straight and strong.

Now turn your awareness to your legs. Feel them long and strong, standing straight but without locking your knees. Become aware of the slight curve behind your knees, the lightly curving space between your legs, your knees feeling free and loose, facing outwards over your feet, not turning inwards. The base of your spine or coccyx is slightly tucked under, lightly engaging the muscles in your buttocks and lower belly, gently allowing the natural curve in your lower back to straighten just a little.

Now bring your awareness to your beautiful back, feel its width, length and spaciousness, be aware of your lower back and pelvis, your middle back and waist, your upper back and shoulders. Three open, interlinking circles of space. Enjoy the spaciousness and strength in your back, allowing your shoulders to lower and your shoulder blades to feel spacious and relaxed.

Where perhaps you feel any twinges of discomfort or aches or pains, bring a quality of space to that area, curious and expansive, no judgement necessary. Maybe it's time to have a slow gentle cat-like stretch, all small movements, nothing forced, curving your upper back and shoulders forward and down, neck curving forward and down, eyes looking slightly down, then moving back to centre; then curving your upper back behind you, chest bone rising up, shoulder blades coming together, neck slightly curving back, raising your gaze to the ceiling, then moving back to centre.

Now try moving your hips and pelvis in a free and flowing figure of eight, left hip moving forwards left and back, right hip moving forwards right and back, a few times, or however long you like. Then come back to your centre and to stillness.

Feel your back wide and long and spacious, the back of your neck wide and long and free, your head lightly placed upon your neck, supported without effort, the back of your head loose and light. Let your head move slightly as you turn one ear up towards the ceiling and then the other, the back of your neck is long and free. Bring your awareness to five open, interlinking circles of space slowly in turn, your lower back, your middle back, your upper back, your neck, and your head. Now bring your awareness to the spaciousness in the whole of your back, enjoy its strength and flexibility and the front of your body feels open and free.

Your arms hang loose and long by your sides, and your palms now gently turn to face forward. Notice how you feel as you do this. The area beneath your collar bone in front of your shoulders may feel more spacious, gently lengthening out towards your armpits, left and right; your chest may feel more expansive, and your breathing may deepen. See if you can just let it be. So how are you feeling right now? Notice your thoughts – maybe you're wondering if you're doing it right, maybe your inner critic is criticising your body shape, maybe you're just wondering what's on television. Just notice. Notice any emotions that may be surfacing – maybe you're feeling excited, anxious, irritated. Just notice. Notice how your body is feeling – is there any tingling, coldness, heat, or tension? Just notice.

Ask yourself, where am I holding? My jaw? My shoulders?

My knees? My feet? My lower back? My solar plexus? My throat? My face? Go wherever your attention takes you, wherever you feel a holding or contraction or tension, and imagine giving that place space to breathe. In your mind's eye see the area gently expanding and contracting like a breath. Or imagine the individual cells breathing together, and feel the space both within them and between them, expansive and alive.

Check that your legs are still straight and strong, knees ever so slightly bent and pointing over your feet, which are a little more than hips width apart. Your coccyx is still slightly tucked under, your back still long and wide, your neck still long and wide and free, your head lightly supported, your gaze softly forward, your palms are facing forward. Now let your arms float up to shoulder level, with your palms still turned forward, your fingers feeling light and loose, with space between them and around them. Your elbows aren't locked but loose and free, very slightly curved as if you're hugging an enormous tree. Feel the space in the curve of your elbows. Feel the length and spaciousness of your arms from left finger tips to right finger tips, allowing the back to expand and open. And if it feels

The Standing Star – 1

good then sway gently with the breeze, just like a tree in the springtime with the sunshine warming your leaves.

Feel the space from the top of your head to the base of your spine, the space in front of you, behind you and around you. Feel the space in your lower back, pelvis and lower belly, back and front; the space in your middle back, waist, stomach and solar plexus, back and front; the space in your upper back, shoulders, chest and lungs, back and front; the space in your neck and throat, back and front; the space in your head and face, back and front. Feel the space in and around the sides of your body, left and right. Feel the space in and around your legs and feet. Feel the space in and around your arms and hands. Feel the space in and around your whole body.

Bring your awareness to the space at the front of your left shoulder beneath your collar bone, let it be light. Be aware of the space at the front of your right shoulder beneath your collar bone, let it be light. Be aware of the space in your chest beneath your collar bone, in your lungs, between your ribs, let it be light. If you feel any tightness or tension then bring your attention to it and give it space. You deserve all of this freedom and space. You may feel a deepening of the breath, just notice, no judgement, no need to change anything. You deserve the whole of this breath and this space.

Try saying to yourself as you stand in this position the simple words 'HERE I AM', letting your body absorb the words, feel the power of the words, and repeat the phrase a few times, silently or out loud, quietly or loudly. Or imagine placing these words in your body where you feel strong, or where you notice a need for support, or wherever feels right, just noticing how you feel as you place them. Maybe try placing 'HERE' in the space beneath your collar bone in front of your right shoulder, 'I' in your heart or the middle of your chest, and 'AM' in the space beneath your collar bone in front of your left shoulder. Allow the words and spaces to expand and breathe.

The quality of this sense of space you are bringing is one of power and will, and the energy of this position can be strong. You deserve to feel this strength and power. You are standing tall and wide and strong, taking your space in the world, eyes open, arms outstretched, head held high. You may feel great and have a glimpse of your own personal strength, your will, your courage, your motivation, your decisiveness, your ability to make choices, even if it's just for a moment. Allow yourself to absorb even the briefest glimpse of a sense of your own power and possibility. You may find it difficult to admit that you have these qualities in you. But you do. You have amazing potential. You are a wonderful human being who deserves life and space.

There is no right and wrong in this experience, but as you practise the Standing Star this sense of inner strength gradually builds. The experience can vary from day to day, and you may feel disappointment one day and all fired up the next. Observe what you find and give it space, space without judgement, without striving for it to be anything other than how it is for you right now.

Stay in this strong full Standing Star position for however long feels comfortable. Perhaps only for a couple of minutes, as long as you like. Your arms and shoulders may ache at first, but as you practise this posture and release more and more of the holding in your arms and shoulders, and learn to rest more and more in a sense of your own spaciousness, your stamina will grow and you will be able to stay comfortably for longer.

If it helps, rotate your arms slightly while they are still raised, forwards a few times, then backwards a few times, just for a minute or so, then return to stillness and see if you can continue to feel the spaciousness of this posture a little longer. Or raise your arms above your head and let your palms gently touch, arms straight as you can, stay a moment, then once again return to the Standing Star posture. Explore what's possible for you.

It may also be beneficial to practise this position against a wall, allowing yourself to be supported by the solidity of the wall, to enjoy the feeling of your back expanding and melting into the wall, keeping you tall and strong. Or try imagining that you have a huge hot air balloon inside your body, and allow yourself to really feel its energy and power to support you in the Standing Star. Picture the deep woven basket resting in your lower belly, with ropes travelling through your solar plexus to connect with the colourful air-filled balloon in your chest. Breathe from your belly, imagine the flames rising and allow your balloon to fill with air. Imagine the balloon expansive and free, so big it touches your ribcage and collarbones, filling your lungs and chest with spaciousness and air.

The Hot Air Balloon

When you feel ready to bring this journey to a close, move your feet and legs together, less than hip-width apart, feet face forward, your arms down by your sides palms facing your legs, your eyes are open, your gaze soft. Be aware of your body as a whole being, feel the aliveness within, feel the air on your skin, your feet on the floor. In yoga, this standing position is called the 'Mountain Posture', deeply connected to the earth and standing tall into the sky. It is a little more contained than the Standing Star and staying with this for a couple of minutes after your second space trip should help ground you as you gradually come back to earth, ready to face the world. Then have a really good shake. Shake your arms, your legs, your hips, your feet, or anything you simply want to give a good wobble. Shake out any remaining tension in your body.

You can do the Standing Star as often as you like and for as long as you like. Enjoy it. Giving yourself the opportunity to take this position just once a day for ten minutes can really help you to recognise and access the strength and confidence that's right there in you, even if you maybe don't see it yet. This sense of inner strength and potential doesn't always last,

71

The Mountain Posture

and your inner critic may be trying to knock it down and out of you, but it builds over time so that you find it easier and easier to access when you most need it. Make sure you only do what's comfortable and physically possible for you right now. If standing for ten minutes isn't comfortable, then why not try a Sitting Star on a firm chair instead. The same ideas and guidelines still apply. Just do whatever you can do and enjoy exploring.

6. Spaced Out

I think it's worth mentioning at this point some of the things that can trip us up on our space journey to whole being. As we've discussed, conscious or unconscious suppression of our unwanted emotions or insecurities from both the past and present can be held in our body. Perhaps that holding is reflected in our posture, giving us rounded shoulders, or tightness in our belly, or a frequent frown, or making us rigid and stiff. Perhaps that holding is reflected in the false or favourite persona that we present to the world, or to ourselves, or in the heavy armour we have created to protect ourselves.

Fear of what might happen if we give ourselves space to feel and to be ourselves leads us to try and avoid our feelings, and resist a true connection with our bodies. Maybe it doesn't seem safe, and maybe we are scared of what might happen if we change. Maybe we're afraid that allowing ourselves to feel our loneliness or anger or grief or anxiety or fear of death, or whatever, will be overwhelming. Maybe we're afraid that allowing ourselves to feel our joy or strength or potential will open us to mockery, or shame, or disappointment. Or we tell ourselves we don't deserve happiness, or that life is meant to be a struggle. Maybe we're afraid that the feeling of fear itself will not pass, that we will always feel empty, scared and alone and that nothing will come to replace it.

So what do we do? We try to distract ourselves from these unwanted feelings perhaps by being perpetually busy, by focussing too much on superficial pleasures and pains, and by not truly listening to our own bodies, our own selves. Sometimes this can last our whole lives. All addictions are part of this process of avoidance of feeling emptiness, pain and fear. We are burying our heads in the sand and can no longer breathe. Perhaps this avoidance is a fear of the void, a fear of open space, of feeling too much, or of feeling nothing. We have forgotten that this space allows us to truly feel. It is a space that heals, a space that actually makes us feel more alive and full of energy and free.

There are the obvious addictions such as alcohol, cigarettes and drugs which we use to space out, become numb, and switch off from our bodies, feelings and thoughts. But we can become addicted to anything that we desire – money, sex, good looks, shopping, the internet, computer games, television, work, food, coffee and on and on. The list is endless. We mistakenly fool ourselves that the thing out there is the answer. Anything in excess becomes a way to avoid the space to feel. This is the true void, an addiction to things that are only superficially satisfying and will start to make us feel sick and hollow inside after a while. Addictions always make us feel fearful, empty and alone, even if at first they come with an artificial high. Inside we know this, so we criticise ourselves and to avoid feeling the pain of that knowledge the cycle of spacing out and switching off continues. We go against our inner knowing.

There is no true space in addiction and it is always about constriction in the end, fear of the void, of emptiness. Certainly some drugs can heighten your sensory experience or make you feel spaced out, but you're not fully grounded in your body, in your own self. It's just a chemical high and can never fully satisfy, it always leaves a hunger, a hunger for more.

In our often busy lives and in a challenging world, we're

obviously going to want to space out sometimes, to give ourselves a break, watch some rubbish on television every now and again, or have a drink with friends, lose ourselves in a good book, whatever. And of course doing things in moderation is not the same as addiction. Maybe you need to switch off for a while and just have a good night's sleep. But try giving yourself the space to listen to your inner wisdom and become aware of what you are doing and why. True relaxation is finding healthy ways to keep connected to yourself, spacious, energised, and in balance. Begin to explore activities that suit you, interest you, inspire you, activities that are rooted in our human creativity and connection with nature, like walking, dreaming, nature, dancing, music, art. These make you feel more alive.

The good news is that when you give yourself space to feel, space to breathe, to let your aliveness flow, you connect with that inner wisdom and it always knows what's good for you. The space journey we are on together is a means to bring healing to our bodies by giving our attention, and bringing space, to those areas that we are holding tightly. By allowing holding to ease, and our emotions to release, we develop a sense of peace and freedom within ourselves. We come back to our bodies and begin to feel connected to our whole selves once more. Allow yourself to cry, to feel anger, frustration, hollowness, jealousy, loneliness, anxiety or fear. And know that they will pass. These are natural human emotions that we all share and we need to build a sense of loving compassion for ourselves for feeling this way. It can sometimes feel scary to experience and observe these feelings in ourselves, but we are learning to trust that just bringing space can allow the feeling to release and transform.

The more that you bring space into your life and connect with your experiences and feelings in this way, the more you connect to the present moment, and the less you will want to space out. Your addictions will begin to fall away and the stronger you will become. I know it can feel challenging, but reengaging this connection with yourself will bring you joy. When you have an addictive craving for something, try asking yourself where you feel that craving in your body, and instead of reaching for a drink, chocolate, your wallet, a cigarette, whatever, try to bring a sense of spaciousness to that part of your body. Know that the craving will pass (and this will happen more quickly with practice) as we learn to rest gently and comfortably in our inner space.

Something else that can trip us up on this journey into space is our inner critic or judge. We all have one. That voice that tells us we're not good enough. Sometimes this voice can be vicious, and at other times more of a background grumble. This voice is an echo of past voices or past events, if not word for word then in its belittling, shaming, constricting, choking energy. We often feel the criticism somewhere in our body, perhaps as shame or grief, and just hold on to it. Perhaps we believe that we will never open ourselves up to the criticism of others if we get there first. Maybe we think the voice is trying to help but it limits us so. Holding onto that criticism in our bodies, and continuing to believe that critical voice, keeps us locked up in a smaller world than we really deserve. You're being hoodwinked. The voice is probably telling you you're too this or not enough that, but remember that it's talking rubbish, absolute codswallop. Always. You are simply good enough just as you are.

The inner critic can be quietened by building your

connection with your body, your inner knowing, your sense of space. So, when this voice comes up for you when you're doing the Starfish, or the Standing Star, just notice it with compassion. Oh it's you again. Don't you get a bit tired going on like that? Then bring a feeling of space and aliveness to your mind, don't get caught in the thoughts. Or ask yourself, where am I feeling my reaction to this critical voice in my body? And bring space there. In your mind's eye see the area gently expanding and contracting like a breath, and the feeling will pass. This is the way to quieten that critical voice and connect with your true voice. This is the loving voice you can trust, the voice that has your best interests at heart, never criticises, and helps you make choices from a healthier, more powerful place. From this place we can only do our best. And that really is good enough.

7. Moon Dance

've rather been looking forward to this bit to be honest. Both the Starfish and the Standing Star offer an opportunity to explore the spaciousness within our bodies, to begin to bring love and acceptance to your human being-ness, to feel a connection with your own power and potential. You're getting good at listening to your body. So how about letting your body move a little, give it a bit more room to express what's going on inside?

You need to make a big clear space for this, just in case. You can either practise in silence or have music playing, depending on your mood in the moment. My own preference is instrumental music of some sort or another (anything with drums really), as songs and words can sometimes distract your attention from the space within. See how you go. Experiment. No rights or wrongs. Begin in either the Starfish or the Standing Star position and turn your attention inwards. Become aware of the space within your body in its wholeness. Feel its tingling aliveness.

Bring your awareness to anywhere in your body where you feel holding, and imagine giving that area space to breathe. Let it be expansive, spacious and alive. From that feeling is there a movement? Let that part of you move. Maybe a tiny jerking movement. Maybe a large flowing movement. Whatever feels right. With your inner eye see if there is any other place where there is tension or holding, or maybe life and excitement, and bring the quality of spaciousness there. From that feeling is there a movement? Let that part of you move.

Maybe you're lying on the floor in the Starfish and you start to let your right arm gently move, in the air, down by your side, wherever, however you like. No need to stay in the Starfish shape. Do your shoulders want to roll against the floor? Do your legs want to wave in the air? Maybe you're in the Standing Star with your feet firmly planted on the floor, and your toes start to tap. Maybe your feet want to move around the room. No need to stay in the Standing Star shape. How does your spaciousness want to move? Sway, stamp, move your hips in a circle, or in a figure of eight. Move your head, bring spacious looseness to a tense neck and let it free. Whatever. It's all good.

Listen to the music. Where are you feeling the music in your body? Does that part of you want to move, sway, roll, curve, straighten, clench, expand, twirl, wave, stamp, kick, or stretch? Let your body free. Let your body speak. If emotions come up, feel them in your body and move with them. Enjoy the sensation of your body free and moving. From time to time bring your attention to a part of your body where there is a feeling of tension or holding, and bring the quality of spaciousness to that area. Let it breathe. Let it move.

From time to time bring your attention to the spacious wholeness of your body and let your whole body move. Dance about the room. Crawl about the room. Roll around the room. Your focus is within while your body expresses without. Remember that as soon as you hear the voice of that inner critic, you must have telescoped out of your body and be hovering somewhere looking down on yourself, so call your attention back within, or feel the quality of spaciousness in your mind, letting go of thoughts, let your head move, let your body move. There's only you, on the moon, over the moon, dancing. Here and now.

The Moon Dance

The Dance

I'm in my body and I'm dancing
In all this space I spin and twirl.
I'm in my body and I'm dancing
My loving heart and hopes unfurl.

I'm in my body and I'm dancing
I feel so safe, alive and free.
I'm in my body and I'm dancing
It's really great just being me.

    You get the idea! Be free free free! As long as you want. Make sounds if it feels right. Sigh, groan, whoop, yawn, grunt, siren, wheeeeeeeeee, aaaahhh, oooooooo, whatever feels good. At some point your movements will become slower and smaller and quieter. Or maybe you've been making small subtle movements all along. It's all good. Your body will tell you when it's had enough and wants to come to a close. If you started in the Starfish, finish in the Corpse posture. If you started in the Standing Star, finish in the Mountain posture, to ground yourself and gently come back to earth.

8. The Starfish Enterprise

Hopefully you're beginning to regularly use the Starfish and Standing Star to take time to focus on how you are feeling inside, bringing a refreshing sense of space to all that you are, helping you fully enjoy the experience of being you. It's worth remembering though that there really are no fixed rules in this space exploration. There is no map where X marks the spot of the buried treasure. You are the captain of your own space ship and are free to explore wherever your instinct takes you. Give yourself permission to have some fun with it. Trust yourself. There are loads of other ways to help access the feeling of spaciousness within you while you're in the basic postures. See what works. So here a few more ideas to play with. Maybe some will help and others won't do it for you, remember your own journey is unique.

Words are very powerful triggers for the body and emotions. Try experimenting with positive words or phrases. For example, when you are focussing your attention on a part of your body where there is tension or holding, bringing a feeling of spaciousness, perhaps bring also a single word with a spacious quality such as simply 'free'. Repeat the word silently or quietly to yourself, lengthen it, enjoy the feel of it and let it permeate that part of you. Absorb the quality of the word. Stay with the feeling a while. See if the experience of space deepens. Just notice your reaction. No judgement. If it causes more constriction or holding then that's not the word for you. If the word feels right, then repeat the word while focussing your attention on the spaciousness of your whole body, and absorb its spacious quality. See if your experience changes or deepens.

Maybe try other words like 'love' or 'air' or 'space' or 'warmth' or 'coolness' or 'breath' or 'peace' or 'joy'. Whatever has the quality of spacious acceptance for you. Or maybe try short phrases like 'I am safe' or 'I accept myself' or 'I am here' or 'I am me', which can be helpful in the Starfish. Or try phrases like 'I am great!' or 'I can choose' or 'Here I am' in the Standing Star. Really feel them and notice what energy they have for you and how they fill or expand the space within you.

Pure sounds as well as words can be powerful and freeing for our cells and whole being, and can bring that quality of space we're looking for, especially open vowel sounds like 'aaaaaaaahhhh' or 'ooooooooohhh', but also sounding consonants like 'mmmmmmmmmmmmmmmm' or 'sssssssssssssss'. These sounds can help release any constriction or tension and allow expression of any emotions we may be feeling. The open vowel sounds are particularly helpful in the Starfish position.

Adding consonants to vowels brings a different quality to the sound and the vibration of the sound in the spaces of the body. For example, try adding an 'h' to the vowel sounds like 'hhaaaaaaaahhhh' or 'hhooooooohhh' in the Standing Star position for a sense of strength and determination. Experiment with other sounds like 'vvvaaaaaaahh' or 'yyuuuuuummmmmm' or 'hheeeeeeeeeeeeeee'. Even if you are silently imagining making these sounds you will notice a shift in the sensation of spaciousness in the body.

Opening to vibrations of sound is important in the ancient practice of chanting, and in the yoga tradition key sounds or

Chakra Spaces

mantras are related to the energy centres of the body known as chakras. The seven chakras are the root (first – located at base of the spine), the lower belly (second – beneath the belly button), the solar plexus (third), heart (fourth), throat (fifth), third eye (sixth – located between the eyebrows) and the crown (seventh – located at the top of the head).

This may be something you are interested to explore, and traditionally these energy centres are associated with different emotions and aspects of human nature. For this space journey though it is simply useful to think of these areas as seven circles of spaciousness in the body. In the Starfish or Standing Star positions try bringing your awareness to each of these circles in turn, imagining them as interlinking balls of energy within your body, and bringing a sense of spacious aliveness to each from first to seventh and from seventh to first.

You can also try out the sounds associated with each of the chakra spaces which are Lam (first), Vam (second), Ram (third), Yam (fourth), Ham (fifth), Om or Aum (sixth and seventh). Whether you are imagining the sound or making the sound out aloud, lengthen the sounds, 'laaahhhhmmm' or 'ooooommmm'

The Inner Smile

(the 'o' sound here is as in the name 'home'), and let yourself really feel the sounds filling each of the spaces, noticing and opening to any vibrations you are feeling in your body. No right or wrong. Just the freedom to explore space.

Another simple way of opening to the sense of expansion and spaciousness in your body is to imagine an inner smile. Turn your attention inwards and ask you yourself where am I holding? Perhaps you are holding tension between your eyebrows and frowning, so imagine an inner smile right there inside the space between your eyes, letting the sides of the mouth turn up, happy and free. You may feel your breath deepen slightly and a release in the tension, just notice. Or perhaps you are holding tension in your solar plexus, again imagine an inner smile inside, letting the sides of the mouth turn up, happy and free. Wherever there is holding.

Maybe you are holding tension in your pelvis, an important part of the body in terms of our sexuality, creativity and self-expression. Bring a sense of spaciousness to your lower belly, or imagine an inner smile right there in your ovaries, in your testicles, in your colon, in your bladder, wherever you are holding, letting the sides of the mouth turn up happy and free. Seriously! Housing both our sexual organs and our digestive organs and eliminatory tracts, the pelvis is a frequent area of holding in the body. The pelvis or lower belly often harbours emotions like guilt, shame and fear, perhaps as a consequence of social pressures or our early experiences, where we felt shamed or harmed in some way, or maybe suffered painful judgements around our sexual orientation. Sexuality is an important part of who we are physically and you deserve to lovingly accept and express that part of yourself. Bringing a sense of safe spaciousness and acceptance to your sexual self can be both challenging and liberating. Have fun. Smile.

Another direction to take in your space exploration can be to bring your attention and awareness to the physical structure of the body. In the Starfish position, experiment with bringing a sense of free flowing spaciousness to the cells which make up your bones, your muscles, your organs. Just explore. Perhaps you carry a lot of tension in your shoulders. In your mind's eye see the area gently expanding and contracting like a breath, and bring the sensation of releasing and space right into your collar bones, into your shoulder blades, deep into the muscles of your back that allow your shoulders to move. Really explore the physical structure of that part of you, always bringing the expansive quality of space.

Or maybe imagine your skeleton gently expanding and contracting like a breath, giving space and breath to each bone, and to the muscles and tissues connected to them. Or take time to bring your awareness to each of your organs, and give yourself a space workout by bringing a sense of softness, spaciousness and acceptance direct to your kidneys, your liver, your heart and so on. If there are parts of your body which you have health concerns about, then be especially gentle with yourself. You can still bring the quality of space and breath and aliveness to that area, but also perhaps gently say the words 'space to heal, space to heal' to yourself, and allow those words to permeate the sense of spaciousness. If focussing your attention in this way causes you any anxiety then let yourself be aware of it, and gently, gently, slowly move your awareness to the air on your skin, the sounds around you, your back on the solid floor.

Your journey has well and truly begun. Remember that space is infinite and there will always be space inside you to explore. The Starfish and Standing Star postures are a good way to start the journey as they allow us to really embrace our whole space without constriction or limitation. But once you get a sense of your own spaciousness and the freedom within it you may discover others that you also enjoy. Whatever feels right for you.

The real challenge is to allow yourself the time to explore, and to make space in your busy day-to-day life just for you. Always remember that you deserve that space time. It helps to experience the postures regularly, gradually building your awareness, rediscovering your spaciousness, and giving yourself permission to enjoy embodying space. As you continue to explore, maybe you'll notice that you feel a little different one day, perhaps more accepting and trusting of yourself, perhaps more excited about life, or perhaps you will just feel more whole. You can also try a little space exploration when you just need to check in with yourself – perhaps if you're feeling unsettled, ungrounded, overwhelmed or upset, or if you have a difficult decision to make. Somehow experiencing space simply brings a different perspective and helps to connect us with the inner knowing that is in us all. Embrace your space!

Part II: OUTER SPACE

9. The Spacesuit: Journeying in Outer Space

One of the challenges on this journey into space is to maintain and enjoy our sense of spaciousness within when we are out and about in the world. To live a full and fulfilling life, we all need to get out there and have some fun, earn a living, find love, make friends, find happiness, a career we enjoy, express ourselves, maybe make a contribution to society, or buy a dog. Whatever it is that gets your particular space rocket in the air and off the launch pad. But the modern world is a crowded and competitive one for many of us, and it often seems that there are just too many people with not enough space. And how on earth do we keep this connection with our inner selves when we have to put up with aliens?

Relationships can be demanding and we can often lose ourselves in them. They all make demands on our time, emotional energy, physical energy, money, and our senses. And don't forget, hard as it is to believe, we make similar demands on others. This applies not only to our relationships with the people we love, our partners, family, friends; but also the people we work with for forty hours a week; or even the people we come into contact with when we carry on our day to day lives, travelling to work, doing the shopping, having a night out, everywhere we go. Unless we live the isolated existence of the hermit on a mountain top or make a move to some distant planet, then we need to learn how to rub along with our fellow man. We share our world, and the human being is fundamentally a social animal, with an innate sense of community and shared experience. The good news is that the more we are in touch with and allow our own spaciousness, the healthier and more nourishing our relationships become. They stimulate and energise us rather than drain and diminish us.

In some ways becoming more spacious in our way of being heightens our senses. We become more aware of what is happening within us, and we become more sensitive to our surroundings and how things impact upon us. This very awareness empowers us to make healthier choices for ourselves where we can. But we can't always choose who we come into contact with on a day to day basis. Neither can we control how others behave around us, not even our nearest and dearest. Yet even amidst the rush and noise of the city, or the clamour of the family home, we can maintain our sense of inner spaciousness, and just let the world flow around and through us.

We often try and cope with this outside world by holding on tight. We hunch our shoulders and tense our bodies as we go about our daily lives, protecting ourselves from unwanted interactions by shutting down our senses or spacing out and switching off. Maybe we make ourselves physically small in our posture, so we don't get noticed or get in anyone's way. Or adopt a false joviality or devil may care attitude. Maybe we make ourselves physically large and imposing, with a stern look upon on our face so that no one dares to get in our way. Perhaps we clamp headphones to our ears on the journey to work to block out the annoying person shouting into a mobile phone, or glue our eyes to a book to avoid a conversation with a stranger on the train. Perhaps we grit our teeth and swallow our irritation when someone in the supermarket

The Suit of Armour in Outer Space

jumps the queue. Or perhaps we hold our breath to hide our anger and hurt when our boss or our partner is overbearing or insensitive. This behaviour becomes our suit of armour. It's all an act, a defence against the outside world, and it causes a rigidity or tension in our bodies because it's not a true embodiment of our own inner spaciousness.

The trouble is our defensive emotional reactions to all the little things we face every day cause a build up of holding and tension in our bodies. Bit by bit we lose our sense of inner space and instead feel more and more constricted. Thankfully, this is where all our practice with the Starfish and the Standing Star comes in handy. We know how it is to feel spacious inside. So go there! Remember how it physically feels to stand in the Standing Star and allow your body to really feel that sense of spaciousness wherever you are. Your body responds immediately to the power of your imagination.

Wherever you are you can become aware of where the tension is building and give it space. Imagine the cells in that part of your body gently pulsating, gently expanding and contracting, spacious and free. Just lightly observe any emotions that are

The Secret Star

coming up in you, maybe irritation, or anxiety, or compassion, or pity, or hatred, or jealousy, or frustration. Just notice. You don't have to act on them. Your breath may calm and deepen. Keep focussing on the spaciousness within you and it will just flow over and through you. Sounds, images, emotions, don't hold on to them, just let them flow. When you are in touch with your inner space, even if it's just for a moment, there is nothing but flow. This is the Secret Star. You can do it anywhere, anytime. Even if it's just for a moment. Why build up all the tension in your body over the day only to take it home with you?

It's an unfortunate and inconvenient truth, but we can't change how other people behave. We share our world, but we each have our own individual universes to explore, with our own histories, and we're all just trying to make sense of our own lives and to take our rightful space. Trouble is it might feel sometimes like people are trying to take yours, and that can be difficult to handle, making us grumpy, sad, or stressed and anxious. And it's true some people can be space invaders. Perhaps they are demanding, taking out their own troubles on you, or perhaps they have a poor emotional awareness in the sense that they have no idea how they impact on others. Don't take it personally. Only you can control your inner space and actively make the choice to keep it free, expansive, and alive. You can choose not to let your inner space be invaded. Remember we can always come back to the spaciousness within us, and we can always choose not to take other people's behaviour personally. Practise your Secret Star, check in with your inner space, and just let other people's stuff flow over you. Don't hold on to it. It's not yours. You are only responsible for exploring your own universe.

If we try to minimise the impact on us of what's out there by creating an impermeable protective shell, this affects us physically. And as we've seen, it can cause us to hold our breath, hunch our shoulders, numb our senses, and create tension in our bodies. This approach can certainly work to a degree, but because it is not a spacious state of being, it also has the downside of shutting out the positive connections we might experience day to day along with the negative. We throw the baby out of the space rocket with the bathwater so to speak.

Yet if we can remain aware of our inner space while in

outer space, we stay open to what's out there. We are more likely to enjoy feeling the sun on our faces, the wind in our hair, to hear beauty in birdsong and traffic noise, to feel alive with the buzz of shared humanity around us. We are more likely to notice the genuine smile of a passerby, to get pleasure passing the time of day with a shop assistant, to feel gratitude for a small kindness of a colleague, or to notice that the boss at work can be quite funny sometimes when you get to know them. Whatever it might be, just allow yourself to notice the simple pleasures of day to day living. When something impacts on you, check in with your inner space, notice if you're feeling joy, excitement, the warmth of companionship, let yourself feel it and then simply let it flow through you. No need to try and hang on to it. There's plenty more where that came from.

It's a gamble though, isn't it? Being in outer space can bring both pleasure and pain. But the more we become aware of our inner spaciousness, the more we can consciously choose how to respond to events. And for added support and comfort, try wearing your spacesuit when you're out and about, and get rid of that old clunky suit of armour you've been wearing.

The Spacesuit in Outer Space

It's so last season. Imagine this spacesuit is made just for you. Its fine, silvery-white fabric is strong and supple, smooth to the touch, porous and breathable. It reminds you to bring your awareness to your inner spaciousness, to take your space, and it supports you, wherever you are. It filters out the negative connections, allows you not to take things personally, not to let other people's words hurt you, so they just flow over you. And at the same time it lets the positive connections touch your heart, they flow through you, and you get to smell the roses, hear the music, and feel the joy of the dance of life. It really is made of clever stuff that spacesuit of yours. Picture it. Feel the fabric on your skin. And wear it with pride.

10. The Friendly Star

Being our true spacious selves when we're with other people can certainly be challenging. It can take a bit of time and practice to begin to change years of adapting ourselves (consciously or unconsciously) to suit others; or to suit our own perception of what others think or require of us; or to suit how we think we should be and behave. The dynamics of certain relationships can lead us to change our behaviour and mask our emotions rather than be true to how we honestly feel inside. Perhaps you present yourself as strong and confident with your partner, when really you would like more support and kindness. Perhaps you make yourself smaller than you are with your friends, staying quietly in the background whilst letting your opinions and passions go unvoiced and unheard.

The key to unlocking your true and spacious self is to focus on feeling the spaciousness inside – both when you're on your own, and when you are in relationship with others.

Bringing your awareness to what is happening within allows you to acknowledge and honour what you think and feel, and enables you to make a conscious choice to be true to yourself, and to connect authentically with others. To be honest, you can ignore all the wordy bits in this book and just focus on feeling spacious inside. It can be as simple as that if we let it. But how about practising some space exploration with a friend as a good place to start?

To begin with, take it in turns to be the Star in the Starfish posture while the other person is a supportive Friend. The Friend should sit comfortably a short distance away from the Star and gently read out the travel guidance from Chapter 2, leaving appropriate moments of silence to allow the Star the freedom to explore the spaciousness within. The role of the Friend is not to comment or judge, but to simply read the guidance, to hold the intention of being a supportive observer, and to try to remain consciously present to the process unfolding for the Star. In other words, try not to fall asleep! End this experience with a few minutes in the Corpse posture as normal and then, without speaking, swap roles, the Star becomes the Friend, and the Friend becomes the Star.

Spend a few minutes after you've both journeyed to share how this experience was for each other in the role of Star and in the role of Friend. What was it like being the Star? Did it feel different to when you practise alone? How was it different? Was it easier or harder to focus your attention on the space within? Were there feelings of self-consciousness? Or sadness? Or joy? Or did you feel safer? Or more fearful? Did you perhaps feel less willing to voice sounds in the presence of another? Or more willing? What was it like being the Friend? Whatever comes to you both. There are no rights or wrongs.

Next time why not try journeying at the same time. Lie quietly side by side in the Star posture, fingertips a few inches apart, not touching. If you aren't both familiar with the travel guide, then make a recording of yourself reading it out aloud which you can use to give the trip structure. Or if you've got the idea by now, you can just make it up yourself as you go along. Agree a journey start and finish time before hand, set an alarm, and then each go your own way in your own inner space. Again spend a few minutes after you've journeyed to share

The Friendly Starfish

how this was for you both. Were you aware of the presence of your Friend next to you? Did it change the experience for you at all? Did you feel silly? Did you feel supported? Did you fall asleep?

Or take turns being the Star in the Standing Star posture while the other person is a supportive Friend. The Friend should again sit comfortably a short distance away from the Star and gently read out the travel guidance from Chapter 5, leaving appropriate moments of silence to allow the Star the freedom to explore the spaciousness within. As with the Starfish, the role of the Friend is not to comment or judge, but to simply read the guidance, to hold the intention of being a supportive friend, an observer who remains consciously present to the process unfolding for the Star. End this experience with a few minutes in the closing Mountain posture as normal and then, without speaking, swap roles, the Star becomes the Friend, and the Friend becomes the Star.

Once again, spend a few minutes after you've both journeyed to share how this experience was for you in the role of Star and in the role of Friend. What was it like being the Star? Did it feel different to when you practise alone? How was it different? Was it easier or harder to focus your attention on the space within? Were there feelings of self-consciousness? Of anger? Of humour? Of shame? Did you feel safer? Or more fearful? What other feelings came up for you? Did you feel trusting of your Friend? Or suspicious of judgement? Did you feel more powerful? Or less powerful? What was it like being the Friend? Whatever comes to you both. There are no rights or wrongs.

When it feels right, perhaps you could try journeying in the Standing Star at the same time too. As before, use a recording of yourself reading the travel guidance out aloud if it helps, or agree to a fixed journey time beforehand (so that you both know you will be standing for a full ten minutes or whatever) and then each go your own way in your own inner space. Begin standing back to back, with the area between your shoulder blades (the lower part of your upper back which is your heart area) lightly touching if possible, although obviously the extent to which your backs meet and where they meet will depend on your height differences. Try not to lean into each

The Friendly Standing Star

other, although it may be tempting, but just lightly meet each other. Or, if you like, do a quick back to back wriggle to start off, like bears scratching an itch against a tree. Perhaps you'll find you go through the three stages of the Standing Star at different speeds, depending on how long you can stay in the full Standing Star with your arms raised, but it doesn't matter. It's ok to stay in the Mountain posture arms lowered while your Friend shows off their stamina.

Finish when you have both had some time in the Mountain posture. As before, spend a few minutes after you've journeyed to share how this was for you both. Was the presence of your Friend a support? Or a distraction? Did it make it more difficult to focus on your inner spaciousness? Was it more enjoyable? Did you enjoy a sense of supporting your Friend? Maybe you felt as though your space merged with the space of your Friend? Did being back to back change the quality of the Standing Star experience for you? Was it less or more powerful? How was it different?

And then, if you feel like it, do the Moon Dance together and let it all hang out!

11. Space Exploration: Making Contact

O ur relationships with other people can sometimes feel like we're trying to make contact with an alien species. The trick is to learn how to be fully in contact with yourself and your inner space when you're in relationship with others. This same rule applies to all our relationships, even the closest ones, and is more challenging than it sounds, especially if we're not comfortable in our own skin, or we've been hurt in the past. Often in our relationships we find ourselves playing a role to get our needs met and we're too scared just to be ourselves. We don't mean to but we've learned to be this way.

The more trusting and accepting of our own inner spacious self we become, the healthier and more truthful our relationships in outer space become, and the more trusting and accepting we become of others. You no longer need to pretend to be someone you're not. And the more you know yourself, the easier it is to make healthy choices about who you want in your life and how to relate to them. The more comfortable you feel in your own inner space, the less you will need to look to others for validation, approval, love or security. This is like trying to steal or merge with someone else's space to avoid being in our own. So, as we expand and free our inner space, the less needy or controlling we become in our relationships, and the freer we are to connect with people in more joyous, loving and creative ways. We begin to choose relationships that support our sense of inner spaciousness. And as we start to really believe that we deserve the space to be who we are, we more freely give others the space to be who they are. We gradually become more compassionate and less judgemental of both ourselves and of others. Marvellous isn't it!

Well that's the theory anyway. And even better it works! Changing our experience of our inner space can't help but change our experience of outer space. Try it for yourself. Let's say we've been regularly practising the Starfish and the Standing Star and maybe doing the Moon Dance every now and again on special occasions when we feel like really going for it. Through this we're starting to get to know ourselves, maybe for the first time, giving ourselves permission to explore how we feel inside, just noticing what's there, noticing what we like, what we dislike, without judgement, noticing what feels good and what doesn't, without judgement, and perhaps allowing ourselves to explore and release some of those locked up tensions and emotions in the body. This inner space exploration allows us to see more clearly in our outer space adventures.

Just start to notice how you feel when you're with someone, notice if it's easier or harder for you to stay spacious when you're with them, and notice the physical sensations or emotions you feel. All this information allows you to make a healthy informed choice. Trust yourself. You can work on staying free and spacious when you're with that person because you know it's your stuff. Or you can let it flow over you, or let them go because it's their stuff. You don't have to make yourself constricted and small. You deserve to be expansive, free and stand tall in all your relationships, even when you make mistakes. You can choose to share how you feel with the person, if it feels safe and important for you to build understanding in the space

Making Contact with Aliens

between you. Or you can choose to keep your observations to yourself, accept the relationship as it is, protect yourself and your inner spaciousness. Or you can choose perhaps to simply move on.

So carry on exploring in all your relationships. Let's say you're in conversation with someone and something's not feeling right, you can feel yourself getting tense and uncomfortable. You can do a quick space scan there and then, it only need take a few seconds now you're getting good at it. Check in with where you're holding in your body and give it space. Ask yourself, is what you're feeling an echo from your history which can be released now? Maybe it's an old fear, or a feeling of shame or inadequacy, or regret, or self-pity, just notice, then give it space and let it go.

Or perhaps what you're feeling is an emotional reminder of what you need to do for yourself in the future? Maybe jealousy reveals something you'd like to work towards, or anger reveals a desire to stand up for what you believe in, just notice, then give it space and let it go. Or perhaps what you're feeling is an unconscious or conscious attempt by this particular person to invade your space to satisfy their own needs? Maybe he or she wants to make themselves feel safer, bigger, or more clever. Just notice, don't take it personally, then give it space, let it flow over you and let it go.

If it feels constructive or important then you can actively choose how best to react. Perhaps you can share your thoughts or feelings with that person, and work towards building a more open and trusting connection. Or maybe nothing is clear at the moment, so just notice your confusion and focus your inner eye on your inner space, even while you're still talking!

Remember you can do the Secret Star anytime and anywhere to bring yourself back to your sense of inner spaciousness. In this way, slowly, gradually, you can learn to take your space and know yourself. Even in challenging situations, you can make healthy choices, and your current relationships will become less affected by echoes of the past.

12. Space Exploration: Parallel Universes

I t's true you may meet some challenges during your journey into space, and there may be times when you feel a bit stuck, resistant, or overwhelmed. Or perhaps you could just do with a bit of support and encouragement. Be honest with yourself about this. We all need a hand to hold sometimes, and it can really help to speak to someone else who has experience of this journey and how it can change your life.

In fact there are many other areas of bodywork and therapy which have parallels with and support our space exploration. For example, receiving massage, shiatsu, acupuncture, healing, osteopathy, or practising yoga, Pilates, tai chi, qi gong, or the Alexander Technique, are just some of the ways to help release old areas of holding in the body, develop body awareness, and allow you to increasingly tune into your experience of the spaciousness within. Various forms of individual counselling and psychotherapy, or associated support groups, can provide a safe space to help you understand the impact of your history on your life and relationships, to fully explore and express your emotions, and support you in your journey to take your space in the world. If you have addictions that are particularly strong or ingrained, it is always a good idea to ask your doctor for advice and support.

Many other forms of healthy exercise can complement this process too, like swimming (the floating Starfish can feel wonderful!), running, walking, dancing, singing, cycling, the list is probably endless. Listen to your body, play with it, enjoy it, set it free, but bring an awareness of your inner space along for the ride. Trust yourself to find what's right for you and if something or someone doesn't feel supportive of your journey and your potential, then move on and allow yourself to find something or someone else that does.

In truth, no one can actually do the work for us, and no one can rescue us from ourselves as much as we might wish it. You are the master or mistress of your own universe and that's a good thing, though it might not always feel that way. Ultimately, we have to take responsibility for ourselves on our life's journey, and this realisation can in and of itself unleash our enormous creative potential. But you can certainly find lots out there to encourage and support you in the process. Allow yourself to ask for help, and you'll find inspiration in other people if you take the time to look, it's an important part of trusting and relating to others in outer space. And why not try out some of the other practices in parallel with your own individual space exploration. Give it a go. It might be interesting and who knows where the path will take you.

Don't forget though to continue to make time for yourself and keep doing the Starfish, the Standing Star, the Moon Dance and all the rest. You don't have to, but it helps. Most importantly, have fun! Enjoy getting to know yourself and constantly remind yourself that you are worth getting to know. This connection to our inner sense of self, our inner knowing is only achieved through consistently listening to our body, connecting with our body, exploring our senses and our inner space and aliveness. This is why the body is seen as the temple for the soul in certain spiritual traditions. But whether you have a spiritual belief or believe in pure human biology, the body is what we've been given to work with, so give it space and listen.

13. Space Exploration: A New Universe

The more you explore your own universe, the more you allow yourself to feel that sense of spacious aliveness in both your inner and outer space experiences, the more your universe will change. It might feel a bit weird, you might not even notice at first, and yet suddenly or gradually you will realise you are making different choices for yourself. You are starting to accept how you feel and who you are, and to believe that you have as much right to take and enjoy your space as anyone else. As you begin to explore this new version of your universe, you will begin to enjoy your rediscovered spaciousness, and start to fill that space in ways that are more positive and nurturing.

When you really listen to your body and give it space it becomes much harder to do the things you used to do to keep yourself small and constricted. As you clear the space of all your old self-judgements and habits, you'll find a much more creative space to explore. Perhaps it will feel quite childlike and innocent, allow yourself to play. Perhaps you will begin to find humour, absurdity or pathos in the life and situations you find yourself in, allow yourself to laugh, allow yourself to cry. Perhaps you become more open and compassionate with other people, allow yourself to be vulnerable and to truly connect. Find things that interest you and use your mind. Find things to be passionate about and express your feelings. Find ways to move and listen to your body, open to your five senses of sight, sound, touch, smell and taste, enjoy moving in your space and express your aliveness.

When you truly listen to your body and feel the space alive within it, you'll notice when certain foods, or places, or people, or habits cause constriction rather than space, and begin to change naturally. It won't feel like an effort. You have as much right to take your space and express yourself as anyone else. As you listen to your body more and more often, begin to notice what makes you feel truly spacious. Doing the work you love? Being by the sea? Starting a new business? Being in nature? Spending time with your family? Playing music? Dancing?

Painting? Singing? Do more of it! Whatever it is for you as long as it makes you feel good. No need for artificial highs to enjoy this new found sense of freedom.

Connecting with beauty can make us feel spacious too if we take the time to appreciate a flower or a tree, an inspiring view, a painting, a sculpture, a lived-in face, a child's laugh, a hard-working hand, or a piece of music. Everything has its own beauty, and giving it space and attention changes the experience and can deepen your appreciation. What people and places are you drawn to? What activities are you drawn to? Maybe you could give it a go? Listen to yourself, trust yourself, and explore those undiscovered corners of your universe.

Epilogue: Back to Earth

So now you're free to go off and explore your entire universe. And just to confuse you, let me tell you that the journey has no beginning and no end, but the universe is infinite. Enjoy! Send me a postcard! Make sure you remember to bring freedom and spaciousness to your inner space and outer space, but don't forget to keep your feet on this solid Earth. Dance!

I hope you find some of the simple tools in this book useful on your journey of space exploration. Using them will help you to rediscover your sense of wholeness, and though there may be a little bit of hard work along the way, you will find great excitement and joy in just exploring and experiencing being you. And when you look up at the multitude of stars in the night sky, remember you are not alone in your exploration. We're all there with you.